For Charlotte Keen and the Ocean Rescue Champions with love – N.D.

For my Dad, who filled my childhood with creativity and laughter and inspired a love of art. And for G, J, A, F and L, with an ocean of love – L.B-S.

First published 2025 by Walker Books Ltd, 87 Vauxhall Walk, London SE11 5HJ

10 9 8 7 6 5 4 3 2 1

Text © 2025 Nicola Davies   Illustrations © 2025 Lou Baker-Smith

The right of Nicola Davies and Lou Baker-Smith to be identified as author and illustrator respectively of this work has been asserted in accordance with the Copyright, Designs and Patents Act 1988

EU Authorized Representative: HackettFlynn Ltd, 36 Cloch Choirneal, Balrothery, Co. Dublin, K32 C942, Ireland
EU@walkerpublishinggroup.com

This book has been typeset in Lucida Bright

Printed in China

British Library Cataloguing in Publication Data: a catalogue record for this book is available from the British Library

ISBN 978-1-5295-2281-5

www.walker.co.uk

The Secret World of
Seahorses

ILLUSTRATED BY

NICOLA DAVIES   LOU BAKER-SMITH

WALKER BOOKS

AND SUBSIDIARIES

LONDON · BOSTON · SYDNEY · AUCKLAND

It's hard to see a seahorse!

Seahorses don't look like other fish,
and they don't swim around in shoals.

They like to hide alone, deep amongst the rocks,
reefs and weeds. Clinging on with
their curly, twining tails…

They can change the colour of their skin
to blend in with the background
and keep very, very still.
Only their eyes move, always
looking out for danger –
and for food!

If a tiny shrimp comes by (their favourite food),
then you *might* see a seahorse move!

Up, down, sideways,

even
backwards –
but
slowly,

gently,

closer,

closer,

closer...

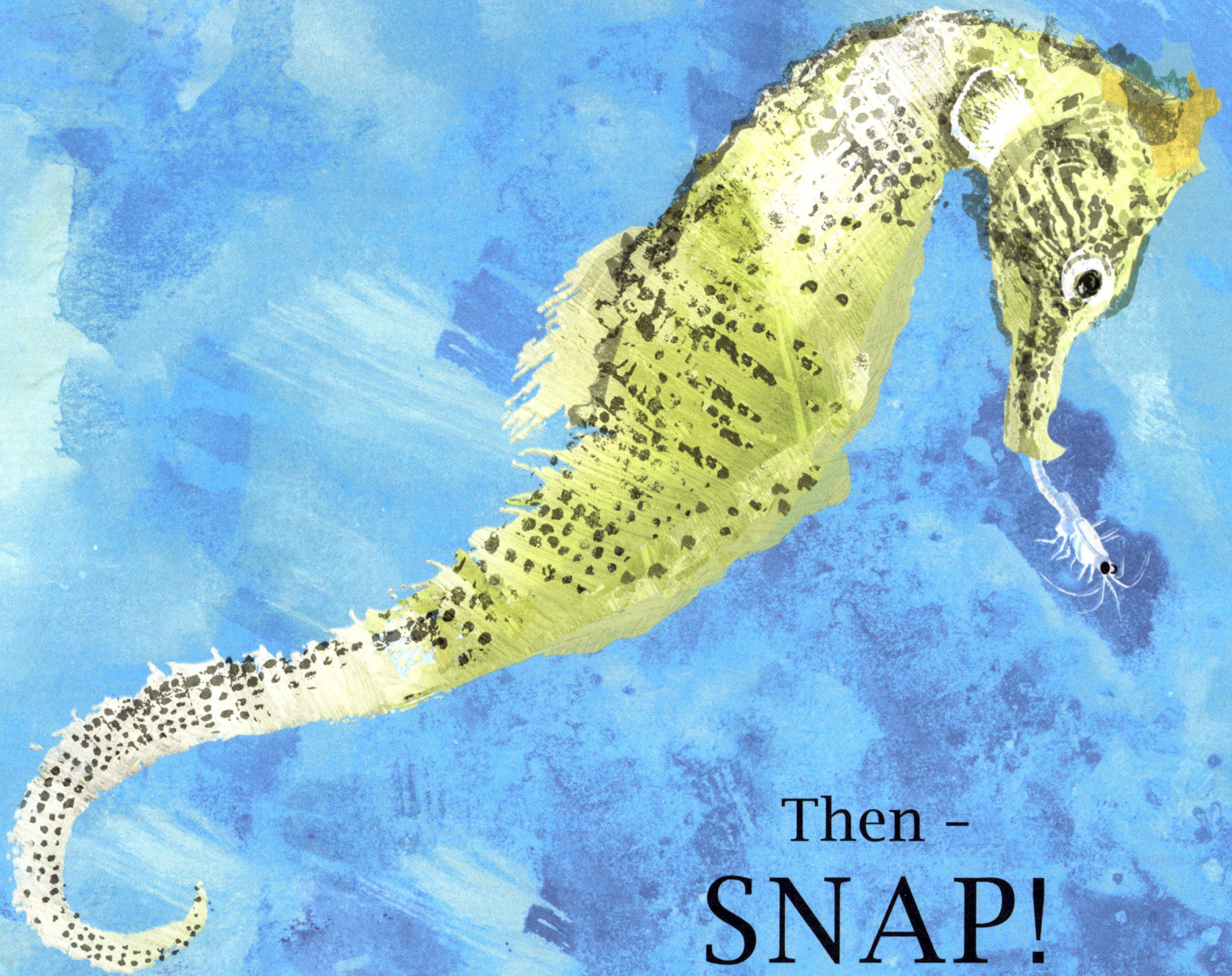

Then –
SNAP!

The shrimp is gone – sucked into the seahorse's mouth faster than you can blink. Eating is the only thing that seahorses do fast!

There are lots of
different kinds
of seahorse.

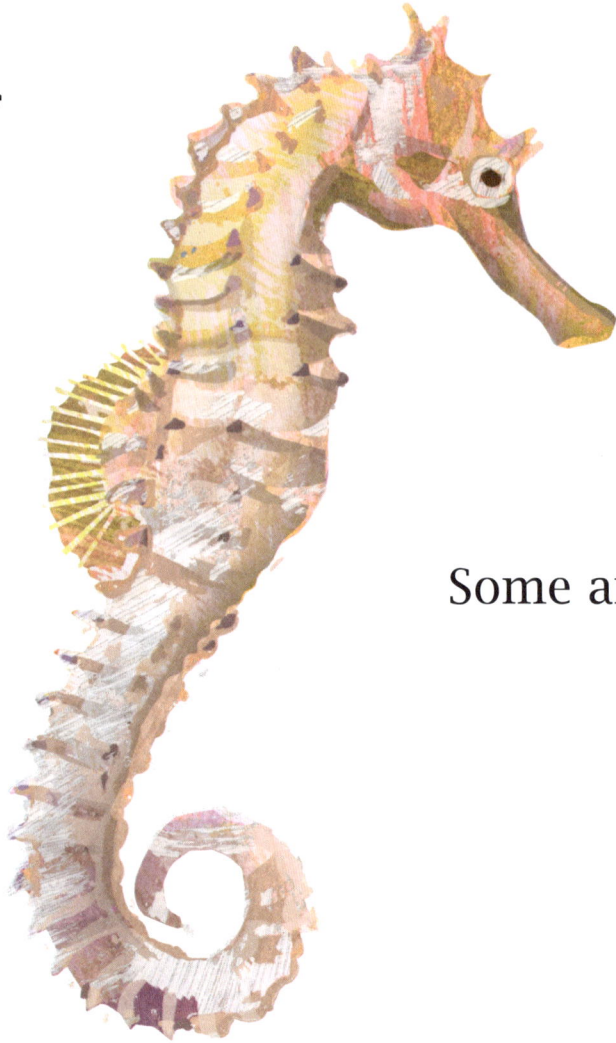

Some are **knobbly.**

Some are **spiky.**

Most are small enough
to fit into your hand.

A few are as long as a soda bottle…

And some are no bigger than
the end of your little finger –
so tiny that humans have
only just noticed them.

All of them are very hard to see,
and not just because they hide away…

Seahorses are hard to see because humans have taken so many of them from the oceans. More than 76 million are caught every year and turned into key rings and lucky charms, or to make pills and potions.

What's more, the places
that seahorses like best -
seagrass meadows,
coral reefs and mangroves -
are found close to the
land, where humans live.

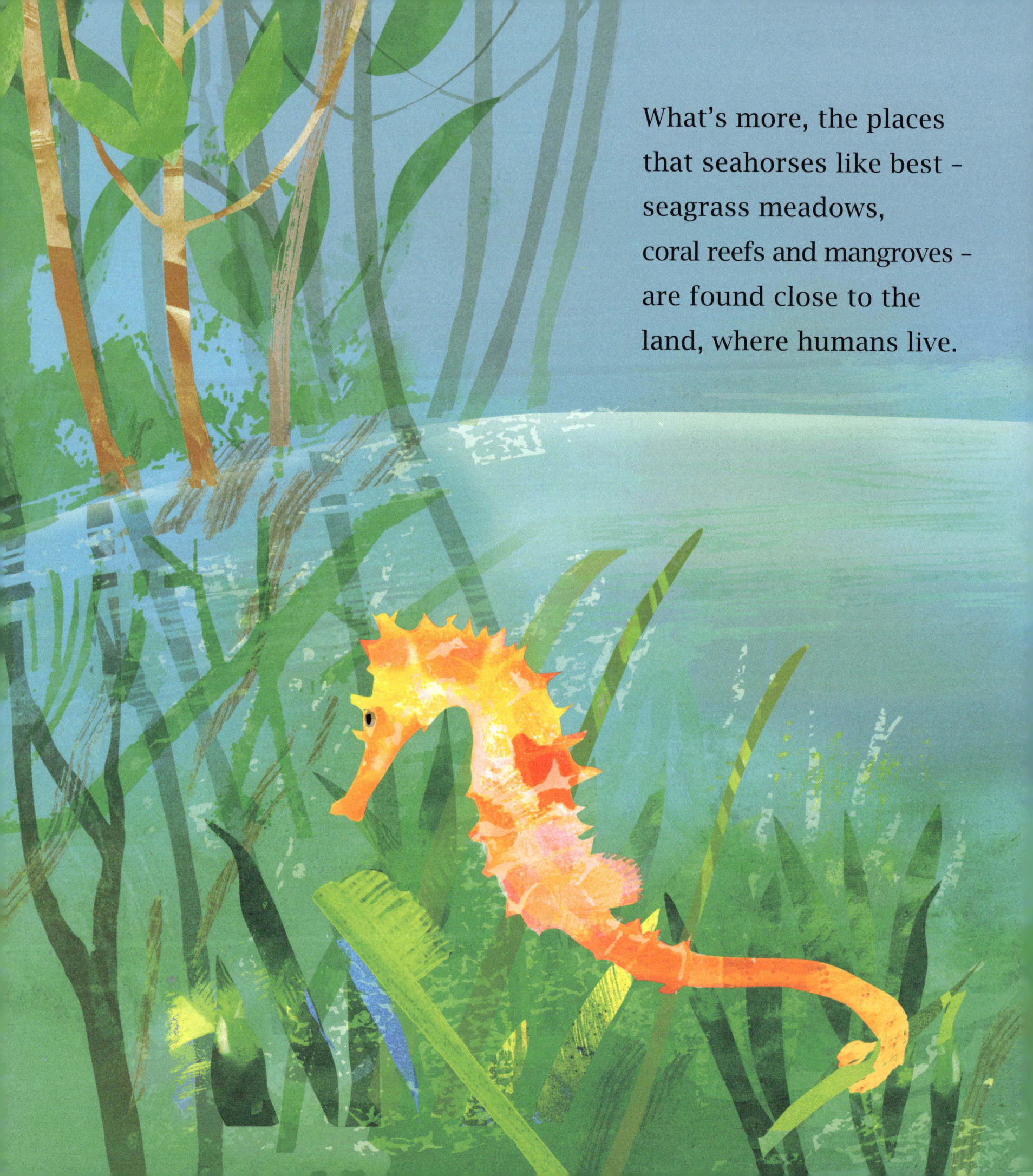

As a result, these habitats are poisoned by pollution and damaged by fishing nets, boats and construction, leaving seahorses with no place to live.

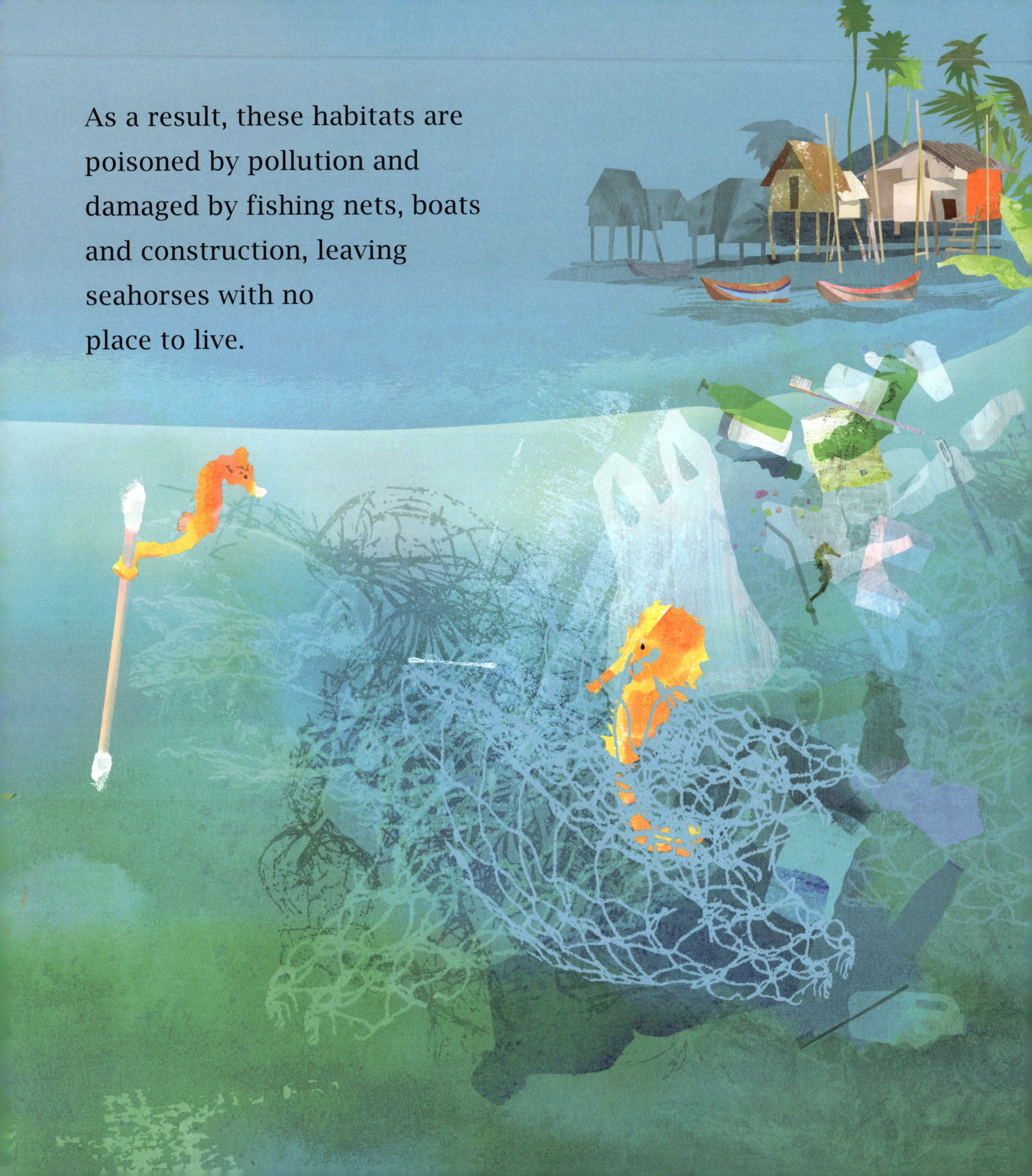

And even where seahorses are safe from humans, climate change is very hard on them. They swim so gently that they can't escape when the water gets too warm or storms become too rough.

But there is hope. Around the world, people are trying to help in lots of ways. In Malaysia, scientists are working with children and adults to tell them all about the seahorses that live in their waters and why they need protection.

In Cambodia, catching seahorses is now against the law. Concrete blocks are being dropped on the sea floor to stop a fishing technique called bottom trawling, which destroys seahorse habitats.

In Studland Bay, in the UK, new kinds of moorings for boats are being used that don't drag on the sea floor and destroy the seagrass beds where seahorses live.

If we can keep the places that seahorses like best safe for *them*, other life will thrive too. And that includes us – because healthy seagrass meadows, coral reefs and mangroves help to fight climate change and fill the sea with more fish for us to catch.

Perhaps then we might get to see seahorses when
they *aren't* hiding…
when they are doing the most amazing
thing of all that seahorses do:

Dance!

Seahorse couples, male and female, meet at dawn to dance together. They twine their tails and touch their tummies … until the female places her eggs into the pocket on the male's round tummy. Then, they each swim back to the safety of their hiding places.

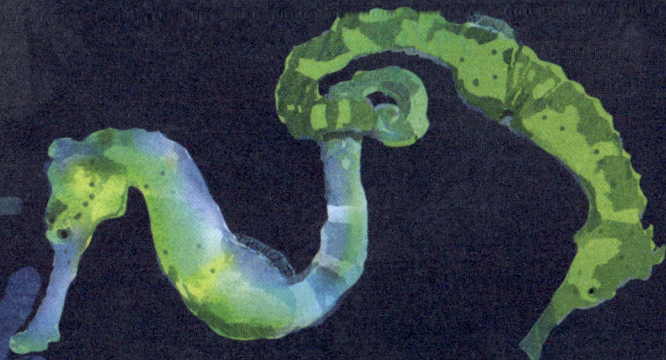

In two weeks or so, the seahorse father
will give birth to a crowd of
tiny sea foals, each ready
to curl their tails,
change their
colours, and
hide away.

Although we might not
always see them, we will
know that they are there.

Seahorses and Climate Change

There are 47 different species of seahorse, ranging from tiny ones smaller than your fingernail to those longer than your hand. Seahorses prefer to live in places where they can hide away, such as coral reefs, seaweed forests and seagrass meadows. Unfortunately, many of these habitats are found close to land, so they suffer from pollution and disturbance caused by human cities, farms and factories. These shallow waters are also the most affected by climate change, which causes the sea to warm and leads to destructive storms. In addition, millions of seahorses are caught every year and sold as pets, medicine or tourist souvenirs.

Given all these challenges, it's not surprising that at least a third of seahorse species are threatened with extinction. But we can still do something to help. Scientists are actively studying seahorses so we know how to protect them. You can help too – by raising awareness about these extraordinary creatures and encouraging people to care for their habitats.

What IS Climate Change?

The air that surrounds you right now is part of what we call the Earth's atmosphere: a layer of gases that stretches from the ground to more than 100 km above your head, and which protects us from the cold of outer space. But human beings have burned so much fuel to make energy to run our homes, cities, cars, planes and trains, that the mixture of gases in the atmosphere has changed. Now there is too much of a gas called carbon dioxide in the air, which affects the balance and means that Earth's atmosphere has trapped too much heat. As a result, the planet is getting warmer.

THIS is climate change, and it's causing unusual weather of all kinds, which makes life more difficult for both animals and people. Storms are bigger, floods and droughts happen more often, and the ice at the North and South Poles is melting, making sea levels rise.

What Can People Do to Help?

All around the world, people of all ages are working to make a difference about climate change. Lots of things we do in our ordinary lives use energy and add to the carbon dioxide that is in the atmosphere … but the good news is, that means there are little ways families can help – things like using less energy at home, by turning off lights when they aren't needed and not wasting food or water.

You can talk to your parents and teachers and come up with ideas together: for example, you could ask if your school gets electricity from a company that uses solar, wind or wave power, or do something to support an organization that protects the environment and helps take carbon dioxide out of the air. Most important of all is to tell other people what you know about climate change and what they can do to help!

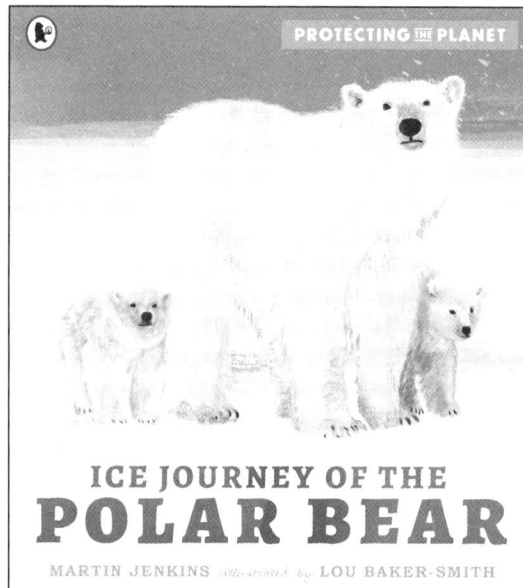